WE THE PEOPLE

CIVIL WAR SPY
ELIZABETH VAN LEW

by Sue Vander Hook

Content Adviser: David C. Downing, Ph.D.,
R.W. Schlosser Professor of English,
Elizabethtown College

Reading Adviser: Alexa Sandmann, Ed.D.,
Professor of Literacy, College and Graduate School
of Education, Health, and Human Services,
Kent State University

Compass Point Books ✦ Minneapolis, Minnesota

Compass Point Books
151 Good Counsel Drive
P.O. Box 669
Mankato, MN 56002-0669

This book was manufactured with paper containing
at least 10 percent post-consumer waste.

On the cover: A Confederate spy watches Elizabeth Van Lew.

Photographs ©: Private Collection/The Stapleton Collection/The Bridgeman Art Library, cover, 31;
The Granger Collection, New York, 5, 12, 16, 21, 24; Library of Congress, 6, 7, 9, 14 (top right),
25; North Wind Picture Archives, 14 (top left), 34; Private Collection/Ken Welsh/The Bridgeman Art
Library, 14 (bottom); Private Collection/Peter Newark American Pictures/The Bridgeman Art Library,
17; Private Collection/Peter Newark Military Pictures/The Bridgeman Art Library, 18; Hulton Archive/
Getty Images, 23; Corbis, 27; From *Ten American Girls from History* by Kate Dickinson Sweetser,
illustrated by George Alfred Williams, Harper & Brothers Publishers New York and London, 1917, 29;
Medford Historical Society Collection/Corbis, 33; Wikimedia/public domain, 36; Elizabeth Van Lew
Papers, Manuscripts and Archives Division, The New York Public Library, Astor, Lenox and Tilden
Foundations, 39; Janet Greentree, 40; Special Collections Research Center, Swem Library, College of
William and Mary, 41.

Editor: Robert McConnell
Page Production: Bobbie Nuytten
Photo Researcher: Svetlana Zhurkin
Cartographer: XNR Productions, Inc.
Library Consultant: Kathleen Baxter

Art Director: LuAnn Ascheman-Adams
Creative Director: Joe Ewest
Editorial Director: Nick Healy
Managing Editor: Catherine Neitge

Library of Congress Cataloging-in-Publication Data
Vander Hook, Sue, 1949–
  Civil war spy : Elizabeth Van Lew / by Sue Vander Hook.
     p. cm.—(We the People)
  Includes index.
  ISBN 978-0-7565-4104-0 (library binding)
1. Van Lew, Elizabeth L., 1818–1900—Juvenile literature. 2. United States—History—Civil War,
1861–1865—Secret service—Juvenile literature. 3. Spies—United States—Biography—Juvenile
literature. 4. Women spies—United States—Biography—Juvenile literature. I. Title.
  E608.V34V36 2009
  973.7'85'092—dc22
  [B]   2008038463

Visit Compass Point Books on the Internet at *www.compasspointbooks.com*
or e-mail your request to *custserv@compasspointbooks.com*

Table of Contents

1

Prison Break

The tunnel was infested with rats, but that didn't stop the inmates of Libby Prison. These Union soldiers were determined to get out of the Confederate prison in Richmond, Virginia. For weeks, using only a chisel and a pocketknife, the prisoners had been trying to dig an underground escape route. Their first tunnel flooded. The second one collapsed. But they kept trying.

If they escaped, they would need a place to hide. So in January 1864, two of the men sent word of their plan to Elizabeth Van Lew. She lived in Richmond, but she was an undercover federal agent—a very clever Civil War spy. Her large house would be a perfect hideout.

Van Lew had turned her home into a hiding place. In her journal, she wrote, "We ... had one of our parlors or rather end rooms—had dark blankets nailed up at the windows & gas had

been kept burning in it …
for about 3 weeks." She
didn't know when the
escape would happen,
but she was
prepared. "We were
so ready for them,
beds prepared in there."

On February 8,
the tunnel finally was finished. It went about 50 to

Elizabeth Van Lew spied for the North in the capital of the Confederacy.

60 feet (15 to 18 meters) under a vacant lot and ended under a
tobacco shed. The next night, one by one, 109 inmates crawled
into the tunnel. It was only 2 feet (60 centimeters) wide and
less than 2 feet high. This cold, dark passageway was their
road to freedom.

Once out of the tunnel, some of the men found their way to Van Lew's house. But Van Lew wasn't there. She was on another secret mission, disguised as a farmwoman with a sunbonnet on her head and a basket on her arm. She was helping her brother, John, escape to the North. He had been serving against his will in the Confederate Army.

When the escaped prisoners knocked on the front door of the Van Lew house, the servants refused to let them in. They

Libby Prison, a converted warehouse, was only a few blocks from the home of Van Lew and her mother.

weren't sure who these men were. Some of the prisoners found other places to hide. But 48 of those who escaped were recaptured and returned to Libby Prison. Two men drowned in a swamp while trying to get away.

Van Lew made plans to get the other 59 escapees out of the South. It was dangerous for a Southern woman to spy for the Northern army. But she was committed to doing what she believed was right. She risked her life time and again and sacrificed her Southern reputation to help unite the country and set slaves free. She would become known as one of the most extraordinary spies of the Civil War.

Union soldiers helped some of the men who escaped from Libby Prison.

2 Southern Roots

*E*lizabeth Van Lew was 43 years old when she became a spy. The Civil War had begun a year earlier, in 1861. Before the war, Elizabeth had led a normal life in Richmond, the capital of Virginia. She was born October 15, 1818, the first child of John and Eliza Van Lew. The Van Lews later had two more children, Anna and John.

Elizabeth's father was from New York, and her mother from Pennsylvania. But the Van Lew children were raised in the Southern tradition. Their three-story house with large white pillars was magnificent. Townspeople often called it a mansion. It was at the top of Church Hill, where only the wealthy could afford to live. At the bottom of the hill was the family's farm, where about a dozen slaves planted and harvested crops. Owning slaves was common in some areas of the South at that time.

The Van Lew mansion and gardens filled a city block and occupied an impressive site—the highest hill in Richmond.

Elizabeth and the other Van Lew children enjoyed many privileges. They took music and dancing lessons, and attended the best private schools. Elizabeth enjoyed reading books in the family's large library. She also liked talking with her father about important national events.

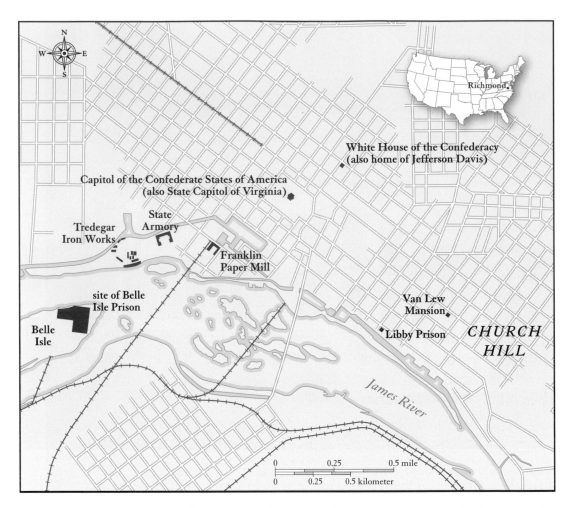

The Van Lews lived near the Virginia Capitol, which became the capitol of the Confederacy during the Civil War.

When Elizabeth was a young teenager, her parents sent her to a private girls school in Philadelphia, Pennsylvania. She found many things to see and learn in the city, which was 10 times as large as Richmond.

Elizabeth was particularly interested in slavery. One of her teachers talked about the evils of people's owning other people. The teacher was a member of the Quakers, a religious group that strongly opposed slavery. Abolitionist groups were forming in Philadelphia. They wanted to abolish, or end, slavery throughout the country. The idea appealed to Elizabeth, even though she had grown up in the South. But the issue was dividing Americans, whose opinions were usually based on whether they lived in the North or the South.

By the time Elizabeth finished her education, she was firmly against slavery. This belief would change the course of her life. Back in Richmond, she often argued with her father about slavery. She begged him to free the family slaves, but he always refused.

In 1843, John Van Lew died. In his will, a legal document expressing his wishes regarding his property, he stated that his

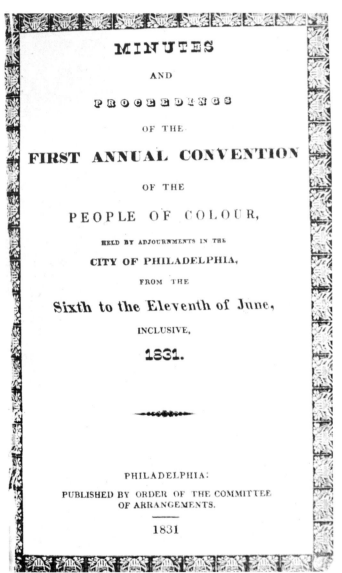

At conventions in Philadelphia in 1830 and 1831, free blacks discussed establishing a colony in Canada.

slaves could not be sold or set free. So Elizabeth still was prevented from legally giving the family's slaves their freedom. This situation frustrated her, but it also increased her desire to end the practice of slavery in the United States.

3

Important Guests

After her father died, Elizabeth Van Lew lived at home with her mother, Eliza. Her sister, Anna, had married and moved to Philadelphia. Her brother, John, was managing his father's hardware stores. Elizabeth and her mother regularly hosted splendid balls and garden parties. Famous people visited them, including John Marshall, the chief justice of the United States, and the author Edgar Allan Poe. Well-known singers and writers also called on the Van Lews.

In June 1851, one guest had a great impact on Elizabeth. A Swedish writer and feminist, Fredrika Bremer, was traveling across the United States to meet America's important women. She also wanted to see what she called the shameful practice of slavery.

Van Lew was glad to take Bremer around Richmond to see

Among the Van Lews' guests were United States Chief Justice John Marshall (top left), author Edgar Allan Poe, and Fredrika Bremer, a Swedish writer and abolitionist.

slavery firsthand. One of their first stops was a large tobacco pro-

cessing company. There they saw about 100 slaves working and

singing. The slaves sang about their joys, but more often about

their sorrows. Van Lew wept, and Bremer was deeply saddened.

Bremer later wrote:

"If these slaves had only any future, any thing to hope for,

to strive for, to live for, any prospect before them, then I should

not deplore their lot—but nothing, nothing!!!"

The fact that her family still owned slaves upset Van Lew.

She couldn't legally set them free, but she told them they could

leave. It was the only way to give them some sort of freedom.

However, Virginia law required newly freed slaves to leave the

state within a year. Because they wanted to stay, many of them

kept living with the Van Lews and kept acting like slaves.

Throughout the 1850s, the national conflict over slav-

ery grew stronger. New states were being added to the United

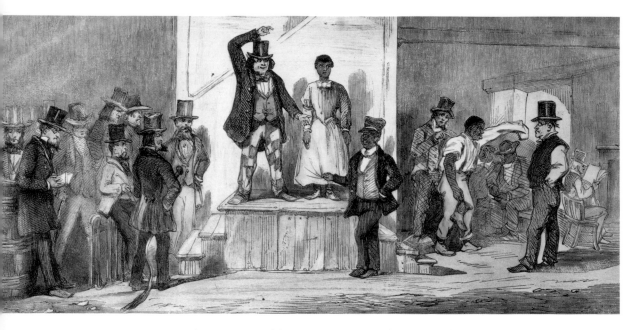

Slaves were sold at auctions in Richmond and in other cities in the South.

States. Heated arguments arose over whether they should be free or slave states. Northerners wanted new states to be free. Southerners wanted more slave states. Some people thought each state should decide for itself. Others thought slavery should be done away with entirely. Southerners argued that their large farms would fail without slave labor. The conflict between the North and the South grew.

Van Lew stood firmly and openly against slavery. It was

an unpopular position to take in Virginia, a Southern state. She wrote in her journal, "I heard a member of the Virginia Legislature say that anyone speaking against it [slavery] … ought to be hung."

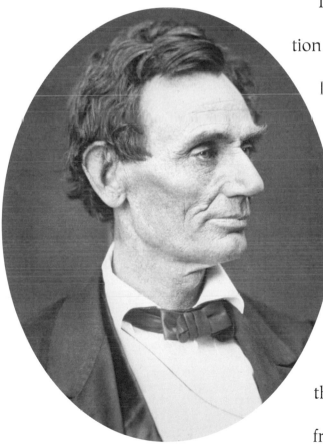

No Southern state was won by Abraham Lincoln in the 1860 presidential election.

In 1860, a presidential election year, Van Lew especially liked the Republican Party candidate, Abraham Lincoln. He believed new states should not have slavery. Most Southerners wanted him to lose. In fact, they said their states would secede from the United States if he became president.

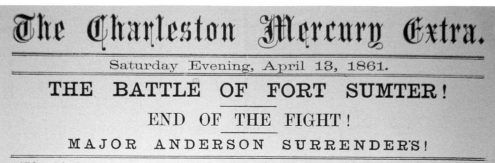

The Charleston Mercury Extra.

Saturday Evening, April 13, 1861.

THE BATTLE OF FORT SUMTER!

END OF THE FIGHT!

MAJOR ANDERSON SURRENDERS!

All last night the mortar batteries were throwing shells into the Fort. At an early hour this morning the gun batteries re-opened their fire, which had been suspended during the night. Major ANDERSON replied about seven o'clock with a vigorous fire. It appeared that he had become convinced that his fire against the Cummings' Point Batteries was ineffectual, for he now devoted his attention almost entirely to Fort Moultrie, the Dahlgren Battery and the Floating Battery. At ten minutes after eight, A. M., a thick smoke was seen issuing from the parapet, and the roof of the southern portion of Fort Sumter barracks was soon in flames. The fire was produced either by a hot shot or a shell. During the progress of the fire, three explosions were produced by the fall of shells into the combustibles of the Fort.

At a quarter to one o'clock the flag and flag-staff of the United States was shot away. For some twenty minutes no flag appeared above the fort. Col. L. T. WIGFALL, in a small boat, approached it from Morris Island, with a white flag upon his sword. Having entered, he called for Major ANDERSON, stated that he was an Aid-de-Camp of Gen. BEAUREGARD; that seeing his distress and the impossibility of his holding the post, he claimed, in the name of his Chief, its surrender. In reply to the inquiry "what terms will be granted," he stated that Gen. BEAUREGARD was a soldier and a gentleman, and knew how to treat a gallant enemy, but that Major ANDERSON could not make his own terms, and must leave the details to Gen. BEAUREGARD.

Major ANDERSON then agreed to surrender to General BEAUREGARD, in the name of the Confederate States, and hauled down his flag, which he had again lifted, accompanied by a white flag.

The batteries then ceased firing, and Colonel WIGFALL reported to General BEAUREGARD, in Charleston.

The following are substantially the terms of the capitulation:

All proper facilities will be afforded for the removal of Major ANDERSON and command, together with company arms and property, and all private property.

The flag which he has upheld so long, and with so much fortitude, under the most trying circumstances, may be saluted by him on taking it down.

Major ANDERSON is allowed to fix the time of surrender, which is some time to-morrow (Sunday). He prefers going from Fort Sumter to the fleet off our bar.

A detachment of the regular army from Sullivan's island will be transferred to Fort Sumter; and one detachment from Morris Island.

No one has been killed or wounded upon our side. A few of the garrison of Fort Sumter were slightly wounded.

The Catawba will take Major ANDERSON to the fleet.

LATEST FROM MORRIS ISLAND.

HOSTILITIES SUSPENDED FOR THE NIGHT.

MORRIS ISLAND, Saturday, April 13, 6 P. M.

A boat sent in by the fleet of war vessels off the Bar, has just been brought to by a shot from one of our batteries. It contained, besides the oarsmen, Lieut. MARCY, of the Powhatan, bearing a flag of truce. He reports the vessels in the offing to be the Baltic, Illinois, Powhatan, Harriet Lane, and Pawnee.

Lieut. Marcy, in the name of his superior officers, has announced a suspension of hostilities until to-morrow morning.

A newspaper in Charleston, South Carolina, reported the Confederates' capture of Fort Sumter in the first battle of the Civil War.

Lincoln won the election, and some Southern states followed through on the threat. South Carolina was the first to secede, followed by 10 others, including Virginia. They formed their own country—the Confederate States of America. Jefferson Davis became their president.

On April 12, 1861, Confederate troops fired cannons at Fort Sumter, a U.S. Army fort on an island in the harbor of Charleston, South Carolina. The U.S. soldiers defending the fort surrendered. The Civil War had begun. Suddenly Van Lew found herself on the wrong side of war. She also found herself in a new country that was defending what she so strongly opposed—slavery.

4 Prison Charity

*I*t was an ugly thing to see Americans fighting Americans. "Surely madness was upon the people," Elizabeth Van Lew wrote in her journal. All states, she believed, should be one country again. She also wanted an end to slavery. But she stayed in Richmond, which was now the capital of the Confederacy.

One by one, neighbors and friends turned their backs on Van Lew and her mother. Some people threatened them. Van Lew wrote, "I have had brave men shake their fingers in my face and say terrible things. We had threats of being driven away, threats of fire, and threats of death."

Richmond was in a frenzy as people prepared for war. Volunteer soldiers arrived daily by train. Women made bandages for the wounded and turned their homes and other buildings into hospitals. Sewing groups made thousands of Confederate uniforms.

When Van Lew and her mother were asked to help sew, they politely said no. Townspeople criticized and threatened them. Reluctantly the two women agreed to volunteer, but they did it their way. They would only deliver religious books to Confederate troops camped near the city.

In July 1861, near the town of Manassas, Virginia, the North and South fought a bloody battle. About 4,700 soldiers on both sides were dead, wounded, captured, or missing

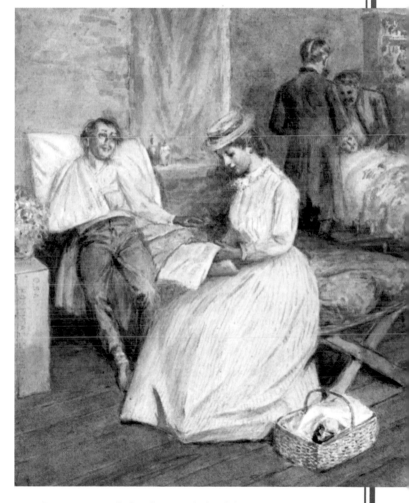

Southern women helped wounded soldiers in buildings that were turned into hospitals.

after what came to be called the Battle of Bull Run. Hundreds of injured troops flooded Richmond. It was a Confederate victory, and the South took hundreds of Union prisoners. So many were brought to Richmond that factories and warehouses were turned into prisons.

Van Lew hoped the Union Army would soon march victoriously into Richmond. Instead, months and years passed with more dead, more injured, and more prisoners. The prisons were overflowing. Van Lew was deeply troubled by the horrible conditions in them, especially at Libby Prison and Belle Isle. She was especially concerned that Union officers were locked up, unable to communicate with Northern forces.

She was determined to get inside and help them. After many requests, Van Lew received permission to take food, books, and other gifts to the prisoners at Libby Prison. But this was a lot more than charitable work. She was, most of all, a spy.

Conditions at Belle Isle prison, which was on an island in the James River overlooking Richmond, were so bad that about 300 prisoners died there during the war.

Her gifts of food and books often contained secret messages, letters, money, medical supplies, and escape plans. She smuggled things under her large hooped skirt or in a basket of food. Books she lent the soldiers contained messages written in code. It didn't take long for prisoners to make sentences out of

Until she died in 1900, Van Lew kept in her watch case a piece of paper that bore her secret code.

the words that she lightly underlined in the books.

Van Lew insisted that the books be returned. Prisoners learned to send them back filled with their own hidden messages. They poked tiny holes under letters or words. When Van Lew held pages up to the light, she could see the holes and piece together words and sentences. In code, she wrote out their messages and mailed them to Union Army officers.

The people of Richmond hated Van Lew for being so kind to Union prisoners. They wanted to drive this pro-Northern woman out of town or even kill her. People shouted names at her and said she was crazy. She played along and purposely acted strangely. As she walked along Richmond's streets, she muttered to herself, swung her basket to and fro, and appeared confused. Dressed in tattered clothes and strange hats, she looked messy. She was a good actress, and people called her "Crazy Bet."

From atop Church Hill the Van Lews could see downtown Richmond, the James River, and Belle Isle, the site of a Confederate prison.

As the North and South tightened security, it became too dangerous for Van Lew to mail documents and coded messages. She started delivering them personally. But it was too much for one person, and she was too well-known. She began using friends, slaves, and freed slaves to secretly carry messages across enemy lines. Her spy network—the Richmond Union Underground—was born.

5

Unlikely Spies

*E*lizabeth Van Lew ran a successful spy organization. The people in it did not seem like spies. One of her most valuable agents was Mary Elizabeth Bowser, who had been a Van Lew slave. Intelligent and educated, she was the perfect spy to go

Jefferson Davis' family lived on the second floor of the Confederate White House. The first floor was used for formal events.

inside the Confederate White House. Jefferson Davis lived there with his family. Many Confederate meetings took place in this large, three-story building in Richmond.

Soon Bowser landed a job as one of Davis' servants. When military officers met with Davis, she overheard their conversations. Whenever she was alone in Davis' private study, Bowser read important war documents and plans. She had an unusually strong memory and could recall everything she saw. No one suspected her, since it was illegal in the South to teach slaves to read. In the middle of the night, Bowser often sneaked out of the house and delivered information to Van Lew or other agents.

Van Lew also had spies inside Libby Prison. Erasmus Ross was a prison guard as well as an undercover agent. Because of Ross, many Union prisoners were able to escape. Well-placed agents outside the prison took the escapees to safe hiding places. One freed prisoner remembered, "Miss Van Lew kept two or three bright, sharp colored men on the watch near Libby prison,

who were always ready to conduct an escaped prisoner to a

place of safety." Many escaped prisoners went to the Van Lew

mansion for refuge. In all, hundreds of them stayed in a secret attic room during the war.

Van Lew also helped people cross enemy lines and escape to Northern states. They often carried important documents to Union officers and generals. These messages were concealed in hollowed-

Elizabeth Van Lew could have been executed for hiding escaped prisoners in her home.

out eggs, fake shoe soles, sewing baskets, and hooped skirts. Some of the most effective spies were women, because few people suspected them of spying. And the female fashions of the day—large skirts and multilayered petticoats—provided many places to hide documents and supplies.

Word soon reached Union General Benjamin F. Butler that Van Lew was a good source of information. So in 1864, he made her an official federal agent, and she began working directly for the government.

6 Talented Patriot

Nineteen days after the Libby Prison break, in February 1864, about 2,500 Union soldiers approached Richmond. They planned to free all Northern prisoners in the city. However, they were met with fierce opposition. Many were captured and taken prisoners themselves.

As the war got worse, Elizabeth Van Lew became more cautious. Confederates were closely watching her activities and her house. Richmond was a dangerous place for a Union spy. Southern soldiers were

Van Lew, a master spy, was often spied upon herself by Confederate agents.

becoming weary of war. Supplies and food were scarce. Van Lew wrote that "women are begging for bread with tears in their eyes." The prisoners in Richmond were also suffering—from starvation, disease, and the winter cold.

In March, President Lincoln appointed General Ulysses S. Grant commander of the entire Union Army. Grant made plans to defeat Confederate General Robert E. Lee's forces. Grant spent all summer battling Lee's armies, which were protecting Richmond. By fall Grant's headquarters were within 20 miles (32 kilometers) of the Confederate capital. But he needed Van Lew's help.

For the next several months, Van Lew's spy network delivered information almost constantly to Grant's headquarters. The spies also smuggled people out of Richmond. Van Lew even arranged for Richmond newspapers and fresh flowers to be delivered to Grant.

Messages from Van Lew and her agents reached the commander of the Union Army, General Ulysses S. Grant (standing, with hat), at his headquarters near Richmond.

On April 2, 1865, Confederate President Jefferson Davis

prepared to abandon Richmond because Union forces were

approaching the city. Important government documents and

gold reserves were taken out of the city by train. Davis and his

leaders also left. To destroy things the Union soldiers might use,

*Richmond citizens waited near the Confederate Capitol after fires
that had been started deliberately got out of control.*

the Confederates set fire to buildings along the James River that

stored weapons, ammunition, and tobacco. But winds spread the

fire into the central part of the city, and people left in droves.

The next morning, Union soldiers marched triumphantly to the Capitol and raised the American flag on the roof. Then they began putting out fires. A group of Union soldiers also went to the Van Lew mansion to protect Elizabeth, her mother, and their home. However, Van Lew wasn't there. She was on one last spy mission at the Confederate War Department building, searching the ruins for valuable documents.

A few days later the Confederate forces surrendered. The Civil War was over. Van Lew celebrated the victory, and she celebrated freedom for slaves. Two years earlier President Lincoln had signed the Emancipation Proclamation. It freed all slaves in Confederate states. In January 1865, Congress had approved the 13th Amendment to the U.S. Constitution. The amendment outlawed slavery everywhere in the United States. Van Lew rejoiced, but the years that followed would not be easy. She would live in poverty and scorn the rest of her life.

Scorned and Honored

Ulysses S. Grant's war successes helped him win the 1868 presidential election.

When the war ended, Elizabeth Van Lew was broke. She had spent most of her money on expenses for her spy network. She had also used her money to buy slaves just so she could set them free. General Grant approved a payment of $2,000 to cover Van Lew's expenses. Congress later gave her $5,000 for her service during the war. It was a lot of money at that time, but it was not nearly enough.

Richmond townspeople never forgot that she had spied for the Union. They never forgave her for betraying her Southern neighbors. Van Lew wrote, "[I am] held in contempt & scorn by the narrow minded men and women of my city."

One person—Grant—did appreciate Van Lew. In 1869, two weeks after he became president of the United States, Grant honored her. He appointed the 50-year-old woman as postmaster of Richmond. Her salary was $1,200 a year. She modernized the mail service by setting up a home delivery system. People no longer had to go to the post office to pick up their mail. Mailboxes were placed at many locations to make it easier to mail letters.

Van Lew served in that position for eight years. She lost her job when a new president took office, and for the next four years she worked in Washington as a postal clerk. When her salary was cut drastically, she returned to Richmond.

With no money and few friends, Van Lew withdrew almost entirely from society. When she did venture out of her house, she was afraid and suspicious of everyone. As she walked around Richmond, people called her a witch and children made fun of her. Although she wanted to move to the North, she couldn't sell her home. The house needed repairs, and no one was interested in the home of a so-called traitor.

Finally the family of a Union Army officer—Paul Joseph Revere—came to Van Lew's aid. Before Revere was killed in the war, Van Lew had helped him in prison. Revere was the grandson of the famous Paul Revere who rode through Massachusetts during the Revolutionary War warning colonists that the British were coming. His nephew, John Reynolds, set up a special bank account for Van Lew. Wealthy people from Boston, Massachusetts, deposited money in the account. Most of them were friends or relatives of prisoners Van Lew had helped.

In late 1899, Van Lew became ill with dropsy, a disease today called edema, which caused parts of her body to fill with fluids. Her niece Eliza, who was living with her, cared for her. But in May 1900, Eliza died unexpectedly. Van Lew was now alone and unable to care for herself. Two other nieces agreed to stay with her during her final days.

Van Lew's journal describes her work as a spy, but only part of it has been found.

Before she died, Van Lew shared a secret with her nieces. Her journal—a detailed account of her spying activities during the Civil War—was buried in her backyard. Her nieces dug it up and brought it to Van Lew. Part of the journal wasn't there, however, and no one ever found the rest of it.

Van Lew died September 25, 1900, at the age of 81. She

was buried in Richmond near the graves of her mother and father. For nearly two years, her grave remained unmarked, with no headstone. Then John Reynolds again helped Van Lew, this time to honor her memory. He had a 2,000-pound (900-kilogram) stone moved from Boston to her Richmond grave. On it was a

ELIZABETH L. VAN LEW
1818   1900
SHE RISKED EVERYTHING THAT IS DEAR TO MAN-FRIENDS-
FORTUNE-COMFORT-HEALTH-LIFE ITSELF-ALL FOR THE
ONE ABSORBING DESIRE OF HER HEART-THAT SLAVERY
MIGHT BE ABOLISHED AND THE UNION PRESERVED.

THIS BOULDER
FROM THE CAPITOL HILL IN BOSTON IS A TRI-
BUTE FROM MASSACHUSETTS FRIENDS.

Thirty-five years after the Civil War, no one in Richmond respected Van Lew enough to provide her grave with a marker.

bronze plaque that said in part,

"She risked everything

... that slavery might

be abolished and the

Union preserved."

Elizabeth Van

Lew had devoted her

life to her country. In the

South she was known as a

traitor; in the North she was

honored as a patriot and

Elizabeth Van Lew set an example of courage and patriotism for all Americans.

spy. She did not consider herself a spy, however. She wrote in

her journal that she wanted to be remembered only as faithful—a

woman faithful to the United States of America and to the idea of

freedom for all people.

Glossary

abolitionist—person who supported the banning of slavery

betraying—being disloyal to someone or something

charitable—done out of generosity

Confederate—person who supported the cause of the Confederate States of America, the Southern states

frenzy—state of frantic activity

inmates—prisoners

reserves—something saved for future use

scorn—treatment of someone or something as unworthy

secede—to withdraw from a nation

smuggled—moved something secretly and often illegally

traitor—person who betrays his or her country

undercover—done in secret, especially in spying activities

Union—Northern states that fought against the Southern states in the Civil War

will—legal statement by a person explaining what should be done with his or her property after death

Did You Know?

- In 1849, a slave named Henry "Box" Brown was shipped in a box from Richmond, Virginia, to Philadelphia, Pennsylvania, where he became free.

- On March 2, 1864, Confederate troops ambushed a group of Union soldiers near Richmond. They shot and killed the leader, Colonel Ulric Dahlgren, and took many prisoners. In a display of victory, Confederate troops paraded Dahlgren's body through Richmond in a wooden coffin and then buried him in a secret location. Before burying him, they cut off one of his fingers and stole his wooden leg. In April, three of Van Lew's agents found the grave, dug up the body, and took it to Van Lew, who gave Dahlgren a proper burial.

- Union spies needed to know whether someone was another spy or an enemy. They often carried peach pits carved in the shape of a three-leaf clover to identify each other.

- There was a shortage of horses during the Civil War. When Van Lew heard that Confederate soldiers were coming to take her horse, she quickly led the animal to an upstairs room in her house. The soldiers never checked such an unlikely spot for a horse.

- Near the end of the Civil War, Van Lew hung a large American flag—measuring 20 feet (6 m) by 9 feet (2.75 m)—in front of her house.

Timeline

1818	Born October 15 in Richmond, Virginia
1830s	Attends private school in Philadelphia, Pennsylvania
1851	Meets Fredrika Bremer and tours Richmond with her to view slavery
1861	The Civil War begins April 12 when Confederates fire on Fort Sumter in Charleston, South Carolina
1862	Begins charitable work at Libby Prison; the work also served as a cover for her spying activities
1864	More than 100 prisoners escape from Libby Prison February 9; some seek refuge at Van Lew's house
1865	Richmond burns April 2
1869	Appointed postmaster of Richmond
1900	Dies September 25 in Richmond at age 81

Important People

Mary Elizabeth Bowser (1839–?)
Former Van Lew slave turned spy; she was sent by Elizabeth Van Lew to attend the Quaker School for Negroes in Philadelphia; she was inducted into the U.S. Army Military Intelligence Corps Hall of Fame in 1995

Fredrika Bremer (1801–1865)
Swedish author and feminist who visited Elizabeth Van Lew; using her inherited wealth, she wrote, traveled in Europe and the United States, and worked to improve social conditions

Jefferson Davis (1808–1889)
President of the Confederate States of America during the Civil War; he lived and worked in the Confederate White House in Richmond, Virginia; although charged with treason, he was released from prison and never tried

Ulysses S. Grant (1822–1885)
Commander of the Union Army during the Civil War; he received the surrender of Confederate commander Robert E. Lee, ending the war; he was elected president of the United States and served from 1869 to 1877

Want to Know More?

More Books to Read

Caravantes, Peggy. *Petticoat Spies: Six Women Spies of the Civil War.* Greensboro, N.C.: Morgan Reynolds Publishers, 2002.

Flanagan, Alice K. *Women of the Union.* Minneapolis: Compass Point Books, 2007.

Lyons, Mary E., and Muriel M. Branch. *Dear Ellen Bee: A Civil War Scrapbook of Two Union Spies.* New York: Atheneum Books for Young Readers, 2000.

McPherson, James M. *Fields of Fury: The American Civil War.* New York: Atheneum Books for Young Readers, 2002.

Raatma, Lucia. *Great Women of the Civil War.* Minneapolis: Compass Point Books, 2005.

On the Web

For more information on this topic, use FactHound.

1. Go to *www.facthound.com*
2. Choose your grade level.
3. Begin your search.

This book's ID number is 9780756541040

FactHound will find the best sites for you.

On the Road

Virginia Historical Society
428 North Blvd.
Richmond, VA 23220
804/358-4901
Contains an album kept by
Elizabeth Van Lew as well as
correspondence and documents
about her life

The Museum of the
Confederacy
1201 E. Clay St.
Richmond, VA 23219
804/649-1861
Features artifacts related to the
Confederate States of America;
site is near the Confederate
White House

Look for more We the People Biographies:

American Patriot: Benjamin Franklin

Confederate Commander: General Robert E. Lee

Confederate General: Stonewall Jackson

First of First Ladies: Martha Washington

A Signer for Independence: John Hancock

Soldier and Founder: Alexander Hamilton

Union General and 18th President: Ulysses S. Grant

A complete list of We the People titles is available on our Web site:
www.compasspointbooks.com

Index

About the Author

Sue Vander Hook is a freelance writer who has been writing educational books for nearly 20 years. She especially enjoys writing about historical events and biographies of people who made a difference. Sue lives with her husband and four children in North Mankato, Minnesota.